321930

Special Days of the Year

Christmas

Katie Dicker

WAYLAND

First published in 2007 by Wayland
Copyright © Wayland 2007

Wayland
338 Euston Road
London NW1 3BH

Wayland Australia
Hachette Children's Books
Level 17/207 Kent Street
Sydney NSW 2000

Produced for Wayland by
White-Thomson Publishing Ltd.
210 High Street,
Lewes BN7 2NH

Editor: Katie Dicker
Designer: Clare Nicholas
Picture research: Amy Sparks
Editorial consultant: Sian Williams

Picture credits
The publishers would like to thank the following for reproducing these photographs:
Front cover main, 11 – © Barry Lewis/Alamy. Front cover inset, 9 – © PIxel pusher/Alamy. 3, 22 – © Hurewitz Creative/CORBIS.
6 – © Liu Liqun/CORBIS. 7 – © Philadelphia Museum of Art/CORBIS. 8 – National Gallery, London, UK, Giraudon/The
Bridgeman Art Library. 10 – www.istockphoto.com/Loretta Hostettler. 12 – © Nordicphotos/Alamy. 13 – Uwe Krejci/Taxi/Getty
Images. 14 – Benelux/zefa/Corbis. 15 – © Paul Rapson/Alamy. 16 – © Profimedia International s.r.o./Alamy. 17 – © Action
Plus/Alamy, 18 – © Betsie van der Meer/Stone/Getty Images. 19 – © Helene Rogers/Alamy. 20 – © SuperStock/Alamy. 21 – ©
Archivberlin Fotoagentur GmbH/Alamy. 23 – www.istockphoto.com/Mike Bentley. 24 – © Adam van Bunnens/Alamy. 25 – ©
Geoff A Howard/Alamy. 26 – Getty Images/Niclas Albinsson. 27 – © David Hancock/Alamy.

Every attempt has been made to clear copyright. Should there be any inadvertent omission
please apply to the publisher for rectification.

British Library Cataloguing in Publication Data
Dicker, Katie
   Christmas. - (Special Days of the Year)
   1. Christmas - Juvenile literature
   I. Title
   394.2'663

ISBN 978 0 7502 5233 1

Printed in China

Wayland is a division of Hachette Children's Books, an Hachette Livre UK company.

Note: The website addresses (URLs) included in this book were valid at the time of going to press. However, because of the nature
of the Internet, it is possible that some addresses may have changed, or sites may have changd or closed down since publication.
While the authors and publishers regret any inconvenience this may cause the readers, no responsibility for any such changes can
be accepted by either the authors or the publisher.

 Contents

What are special days? 6–7

What is Christmas? 8–9

The Christmas story 10–11

When is Christmas? 12–13

What happens at Christmas? 14–15

Christmas time 16–17

Christmas cards 18–19

Christmas gifts 20–21

Christmas trees and decorations 22–23

Christmas carols 24–25

Christmas around the world 26–27

Glossary and activities 28–29

Index 30

What are special days?

We use special days to celebrate or remember an important time each year. Special days can be important to a person, a family, a town or even a country.

In China, the start of a new year is celebrated in the months of January or February. This dragon dance is meant to bring good luck and happiness.

Christians remember Jesus as a baby at Christmas time.

One special day that affects us all is our birthday. This is a celebration of the day you were born. Christmas is a special day. For **Christians**, it is a time to think about the birth of Jesus.

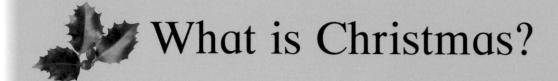

Christians believe that Jesus was God made man. They think that Jesus was born to help people on Earth. Jesus taught people about God. He also helped people who were sick to get better.

Christians believe that Jesus did a lot of good things during his life. In this picture, he is helping a blind man to see.

Jesus died over two thousand years ago, but Christians still think about his life and the time of his birth. At Christmas time, Christians join together to celebrate the birth of Jesus.

Christians light candles at Christmas. This is to remind them that Jesus was born to show people the way to live.

The Christmas story

The Christmas story is found in a special Christian book called the **Bible**. It tells how Jesus was born to a woman named Mary.

These children are reading the Bible with their mother. This is a book of stories, including many about the life of Jesus.

Mary and Joseph (the man she was going to marry) went to a place called Bethlehem just before Jesus was born. Jesus was born in a stable. He had to sleep in a **manger** used for animal food.

We call the birth of Jesus the 'Nativity'. These children are acting out the birth of Jesus in a Nativity play.

When is Christmas?

We do not know exactly when Jesus was born. However, most countries celebrate Christmas on 25 December. For thousands of years, the winter months have been a time for feasting and celebration.

People use lights at Christmas time to make the dark winter days feel brighter.

The date of 25 December was chosen about 1,600 years ago. This made it possible to combine some of the winter celebrations with remembering the birth of Jesus. For some countries, such as Australia, Christmas falls in summer.

In Australia, the weather is usually hot on Christmas day. It is a good time to go to the beach.

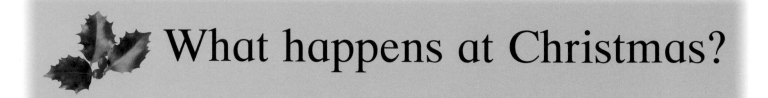

What happens at Christmas?

Christmas is a time for families to get together
for a celebration. Many families eat roast turkey,
plum pudding and mince pies as part of a special meal.

Roast turkey is a traditional dish at Christmas time.

'I love Christmas dinner. It's the only time we have turkey, and there is always lots to eat!'

Sam

Some people go to church to remember the birth of Jesus. Other Christmas **traditions** include sending Christmas cards, giving people gifts and singing special songs called 'Christmas **carols**'.

There are lots of special church services at Christmas time.

Christmas time
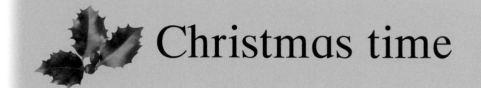

There are other special days at Christmas time. In Mexico, celebrations start nine days before Christmas! The day before and the day after Christmas are special days in many countries.

In Germany, there are lots of celebrations on Christmas Eve. It is traditional to light candles and sparklers.

On the day after Christmas, some churches open their moneybox collections to give money to the poor. Years ago, servants were allowed to visit their families on 26 December, taking a 'box' of gifts. This is why it is called Boxing Day.

In Britain, some families like to go to the theatre on Boxing Day. Sports are popular, too. Some people wrap up warm and go to watch horse racing.

Christmas cards

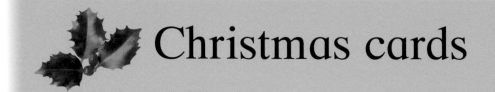

People in Britain began to send Christmas cards in about the year 1840. At this time, the invention of trains meant that people could send letters more easily.

'My cousins live in America. We love sending Christmas cards to each other to share our news.'

Helen

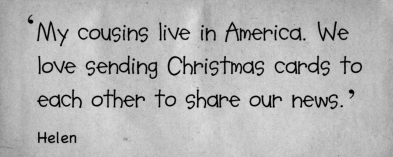

Christmas cards are a good way to keep in touch with family and friends.

Christmas cards always used to show religious pictures of Jesus as a baby. Now, some Christmas cards also tell jokes or have pictures of winter scenes.

Today, there are many different Christmas cards to choose from.

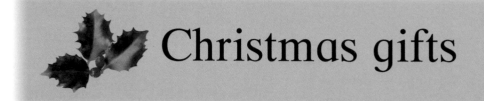

Christians believe that God gave Jesus as a gift to the world. At Christmas, we give gifts to each other.

At Christmas, we give presents to our family and friends to show them that we love them.

In some countries, children receive surprise gifts. Many children believe these gifts are from a man named Santa Claus. Santa Claus has different names in different countries, but he is based on a real person called St Nicholas. St Nicholas lived about 1,600 years ago. He used to give money secretly to the poor.

Many children think that Santa Claus brings presents to them on Christmas Eve when they are asleep.

Christmas trees and decorations

The idea of having a Christmas tree came from Germany. In 1834, Prince Albert brought a fir tree as a present for the Royal Family in Britain. Prince Albert was German and he became Queen Victoria's husband in 1840.

Many families like to decorate their Christmas tree together.

Today, people decorate their Christmas trees with lights and coloured balls. Christmas gifts are wrapped and then put under the tree. Other decorations at Christmas time include branches of holly, tinsel and a circle of leaves called a 'wreath'.

Decorations help to make people's houses feel special at Christmas time.

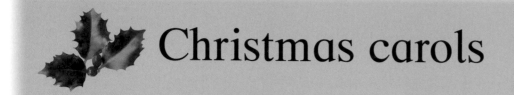

Christmas carols

At Christmas, carols (or traditional songs) are sung to remember the birth of Jesus. Some carols are hundreds of years old. Carols are sung in church.

At Christmas, people sing special songs at church. These boys sing in a choir.

Large groups of people also gather to sing carols outdoors. Sometimes, groups of carol singers gather at people's houses. After they have sung, they may be given food or drink, or some money for charity.

These carol singers have wrapped up warm. They are singing to raise money for charity.

Christmas around the world

Christmas is celebrated in lots of countries. This is because Christians live around the world. Every country has its own Christmas traditions. In some countries, for example, Christmas Eve is the most important time.

'In Sweden, we bake special buns at Christmas time. We also open our presents on Christmas eve!'

Eva and Karin

Many families cook special food as part of their Christmas celebration. In Sweden, families have a big meal on Christmas Eve.

Like Australia, it is summer in South Africa at Christmas time. Many people eat their dinner outside and play outdoor games or go for a swim. During the Christmas holidays in South Africa, lots of people also go camping.

In South Africa, many people celebrate Christmas outdoors in the sunshine.

27

Glossary and activities

Glossary

Bible – A special book read by Christians.

Carols – Special songs sung at Christmas time.

Christians – People who follow the teachings of Jesus.

Manger – A box used to hold food for animals.

Nativity – A word used to describe the birth of Jesus.

Tradition – Something we have done for a long time.

Books to read

- *Gifts at Christmas* (Start-Up Religion) by Ruth Nason (Evans Brothers 2004)
- *A Christmas Story* by Brian Wildsmith (Oxford University Press 2003)
- *The Christmas Story* (Festival Stories) by Anita Ganeri (Evans Brothers 2003)
- *Christmas* (Changing Times) by Ruth Thomson (Franklin Watts 2003)
- *Christmas* (Celebrations) by Anita Ganeri (Heinemann 2002)

Activities

1. Do you celebrate Christmas? What special things do your family do each year?
2. Use other books or ask an adult to help you use the internet to find out which other festivals are celebrated during the winter.
3. Use other books or the internet to find out more about the Christmas story.
4. Make a Christmas card with a picture of part of the Christmas story.
5. Make a decoration for your family's Christmas tree.
6. How many Christmas carols do you know? Learn a new carol and sing it to your family.

Useful websites

http://www.topmarks.co.uk/Christmas

http://www.bbc.co.uk/schools/religion/christianity/christmas.shtml

http://www.learnenglish.org.uk/kids/archive/theme_christmas.html

Index

Australia 13, 27

Bethlehem 11
Bible 10, 28
birth 7, 8, 9, 10, 11, 12, 13, 15, 24
Boxing Day 17
Britain 17, 18, 22

candles 9, 16
cards 15, 18, 19
carols 15, 24, 25, 28
celebration 6, 7, 12, 13, 14, 26
China 6
Christians 7, 8, 9, 10, 20, 26, 28
Christmas 7, 9, 10, 12, 13, 14, 15, 16, 17, 20, 23, 24, 26

Christmas Eve 16, 26
Christmas tree 22, 23
church 15, 17, 24
country 6

date 12, 13
decorations 12, 22, 23

family 6, 14, 18, 20, 26
food 14, 26, 27

Germany 16, 22
gifts 15, 20, 21, 23, 26
God 8, 20

Jesus 7, 8, 9, 10, 11, 13, 15, 19, 20, 24

lights 12, 23

manger 11, 28
Mexico 16

nativity 11, 28

remembrance 6

Santa Claus 21
South Africa 27
summer 13, 27
Sweden 26

tradition 15, 26, 28

winter 12